Contents

How to use this book

Each page has a title telling you what it is about.

Sometimes there is a 'Hint' to help you.

This shows that the activity is an 'Explore'. Work with a friend.

This shows you how to set out your work. The first question is usually done for you.

Instructions look like this. Always read these carefully before starting.

Sometimes you need materials to help you with the activity.

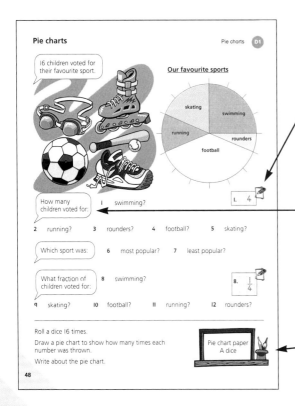

Centimetres, metres and kilometres

Write which unit you would use to measure each.

I

I. centimetres

2

3

4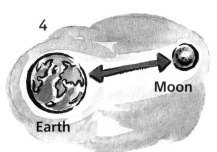
Moon
Earth

5

6

7

8
River Thames

9
DIARY

10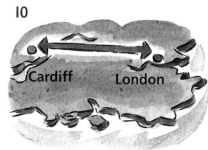
Cardiff   London

Write each distance in kilometres.

II. 6·7 km

II	6700 m

12	5100 m	13	3240 m	14	7000 m	15	9090 m
16	4120 m	17	600 m	18	520 m	19	1100 m
20	100 m	21	50 m	22	5040 m	23	500 m

Metres and kilometres

Write each distance in metres.

1  1·3 km

 1. 1 3 0 0 m

2  4·3 km

3  0·36 km

4  1·2 km

5  5·3 km

6  0·2 km

7  0·1 km

8  1·1 km

9  0·05 km

10  3·4 km

---

Write <, > or = between each pair.

11. 1 m   1 km

II. 1 m < 1 km

12   2 m   2 km

13   6 m   12 km

14   1 m   3 km

15   30 km   10 m

16   1 m   1·6 m

17   4 km   5 m

18   100 m   50 km

19   500 m   0·5 km

20   3·2 km   2 m

Kilometres and miles

Estimate how many kilometres.

1 Dinton 6 miles

1. 10 km

3 miles is about 5 kilometres.

2 Bury 12 miles

3 Newcastle 30 miles

4 Edinburgh 300 miles

5 Coventry 60 miles

6 Exeter 100 miles

7 Cardiff 18 miles

8 Sheffield 50 miles

9 Leyland 1 mile

Estimate how many miles.

10 Paris 10 kilometres

10. 6 miles

11 Bonn 50 kilometres

12 Oslo 20 kilometres

13 Calais 15 kilometres

14 Berlin 100 kilometres

15 Madrid 22 kilometres

16 Nantes 200 kilometres

17 Amsterdam 53 kilometres

18 Lyons 500 kilometres

19 Barcelona 7·5 kilometres

Speed

The distances show how far each spider travels in one second.

Write the speed of each spider.

1. 4 cm/s

1 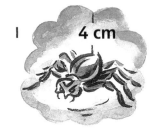 4 cm

2 3 cm

3  5 cm

4 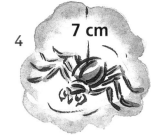 7 cm

5 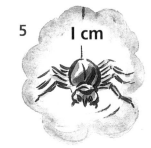 1 cm

6 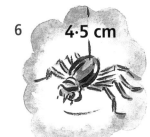 4·5 cm

7 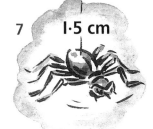 1·5 cm

8 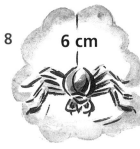 6 cm

---

Write the speed of each snail.

9  12 cm
2 minutes

9. 6 cm/min

10  10 cm
2 minutes

11  5 cm
1 minute

12  1 cm
1 minute

13  8 cm
2 minutes

14  12 cm
3 minutes

15  6 cm
2 minutes

16  3 cm
1 minute

17 9 cm
3 minutes

18 12 cm
4 minutes

Speed

How far does each cyclist travel in 2 hours?

1. 10 km

1  **5 km/h**

2  **11 km/h**

3  **10 km/h**

4  **8 km/h**

5  **12 km/h**

6  **6 km/h**

7  **15 km/h**

8  **9 km/h**

9  **16 km/h**

10  **14 km/h**

How far does each car travel?

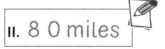

11. 80 miles

11  **40 miles/h
2 hours**

12  **60 miles/h
3 hours**

13  **30 miles/h
1 hour**

14  **70 miles/h
2 hours**

15  **50 miles/h
3 hours**

16  **45 miles/h
2 hours**

17 **30 miles/h
$1\frac{1}{2}$ hours**

Speed

> How long does each journey take?

1
300 km at 30 km/h

1. I 0 hours

2
200 km at 20 km/h

3
100 km at 50 km/h

4
60 km at 15 km/h

5
500 km at 100 km/h

6
25 km at 25 km/h

7
1000 km at 50 km/h

8
125 km at 25 km/h

9
250 km at 100 km/h

10
60 km at 40 km/h

> Estimate how many km/h for each speed limit.

11
30

11. 5 0 km/h

3 miles is about 5 kilometres.

12
60

13
15

14
10

15
50

16
70

8

Volume and capacity

Write the volume of each cuboid.

I
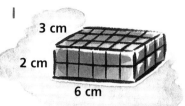
3 cm
2 cm
6 cm

I. $6 \times 3 \times 2 = 36 \, cm^3$

2
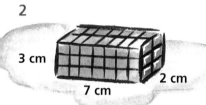
3 cm
7 cm
2 cm

3
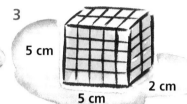
5 cm
5 cm
2 cm

4
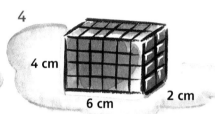
4 cm
6 cm
2 cm

5
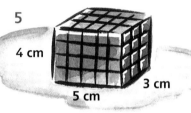
4 cm
5 cm
3 cm

6
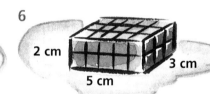
2 cm
5 cm
3 cm

7
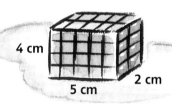
4 cm
5 cm
2 cm

Write the volume and capacity of each cuboid.

8
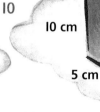
3 cm
5 cm
6 cm

8. $6 \times 5 \times 3 = 90 \, cm^3$
$90 \, cm^3 = 90 \, ml$

q
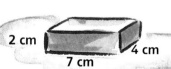
2 cm
7 cm
4 cm

10
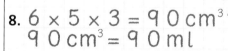
10 cm
5 cm
3 cm

II
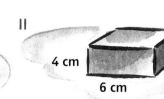
4 cm
6 cm
3 cm

12

10 cm
15 cm
4 cm

13
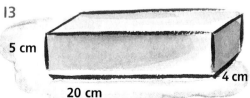
5 cm
20 cm
4 cm

14
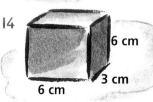
6 cm
6 cm
3 cm

Volume and capacity

Write each capacity in litres.

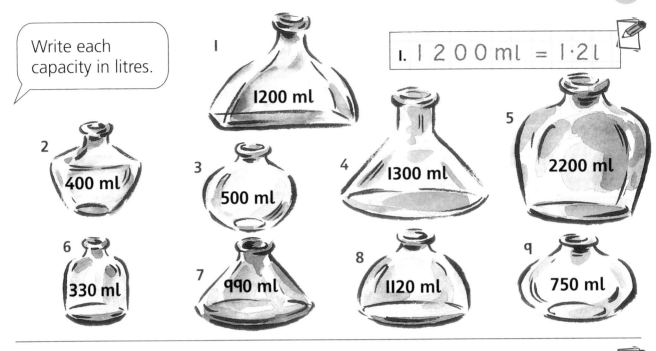

1 1200 ml

I. 1 2 0 0 ml = 1·2 l

2 400 ml

3 500 ml

4 1300 ml

5 2200 ml

6 330 ml

7 990 ml

8 1120 ml

9 750 ml

Write the volume and capacity of each cube.

10. $1 \times 1 \times 1 = 1 \text{ cm}^3$
$= 1 \text{ ml}$

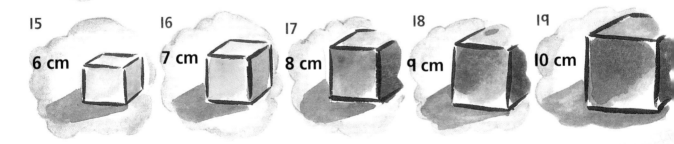

10 1 cm

11 2 cm

12 3 cm

13 4 cm

14 5 cm

15 6 cm

16 7 cm

17 8 cm

18 9 cm

19 10 cm

Explore

Which cubes hold between 1 and 2 litres?

Draw each with its measurements.

Litres and pints

Estimate how many pints.

1

3 l

I. a bit less than 6 pints

I litre is just less than 2 pints.

2

2 l

3

6 l

4

1 l

5

4 l

6

10 l

7

$1\frac{1}{2}$ l

8

5 l

9

$\frac{1}{2}$ l

10

3·5 l
OIL

11

8 l
PETROL

12

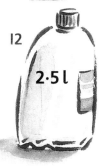
2·5 l

Estimate how many pints.

13 | 500 ml

13. a bit less than 1 pint

14 | 1500 ml

15 | 250 ml

16 | 330 ml

17 | 3000 ml

18 | 125 ml

19 | 750 ml

20 | 2000 ml

21 | 1200 ml

Litres and pints

Estimate how many litres.

1 **2 pints**

1. a bit more than 1 litre

1 litre is just less than 2 pints.

2 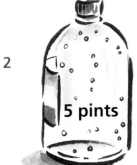 **5 pints**

3  **3 pints**

4  **$2\frac{1}{2}$ pints**

5  **14 pints**

6  **1 pint**

7  **8 pints**

8  **20 pints**

9  **$4\frac{1}{2}$ pints** PAINT

10  **$1\frac{1}{2}$ pints**

11  **4 pints**

12  **$\frac{1}{3}$ pint**

 **Explore**

1 pint is 568 ml.

Use a calculator to find exact equivalents for 2 pints, 4 pints, 15 pints, $1\frac{1}{2}$ pints, …

Write each in litres.

Grams and ounces

Estimate each weight in ounces.

1 **NUTS** 100 g

1. 4 ounces

4 ounces is about 100 grams.

2  **COFFEE** 300 g

3  **Jam** 400 g

4  **CRISPS** 50 g

5  200 g

6  **1 kg DAZZIE**

7  350 g **BEANS**

8  **Soup** 75 g

9  750 g

10  250 g **Tea**

11  $\frac{1}{2}$ kg

12  450 g

Estimate each weight in grams.

13. 1 0 0 g butter

Cake Recipe

1 tbsp bicarbonate

13 4 oz butter
14 8 oz sugar
15 12 oz flour

3 eggs
16 2 oz cocoa
17 6 oz nuts

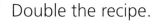

Double the recipe. Write each new weight in grams and in ounces.

13

Estimate each weight in pounds.

1. 2 pounds

I kilogram is about 2 pounds.

1. RICE 1 kg
2. Lentils 2 kg
3. PASTA ½ kg
4. 3 kg
5. POTATOES 5 kg
6. Ice Cream 2·5 kg
7. ONIONS 1·5 kg
8. WASHING POWDER 3·5 kg

Estimate each weight in kilograms.

9. 3·5 kg

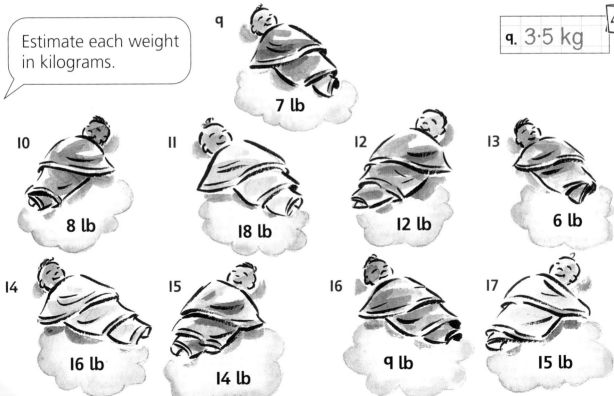

9. 7 lb
10. 8 lb
11. 18 lb
12. 12 lb
13. 6 lb
14. 16 lb
15. 14 lb
16. 9 lb
17. 15 lb

Area

Copy each shape. Write the total area.

I.

$2 \times 5 = 10$
$3 \times 3 = 9$
Area= 19 cm^2

I
3 cm
3 cm
2 cm
2 cm
2 cm

2
3 cm
4 cm
1 cm
1 cm

3
6 cm
2 cm
3 cm
1 cm

4
3 cm
3 cm
2 cm
6 cm

5
4 cm
2 cm
5 cm
3 cm

6
4 cm
3 cm
1 cm
1 cm
3 cm
4 cm

7
4 cm
1 cm
4 cm
4 cm
1 cm

8
1 cm
1 cm
4 cm
6 cm
3 cm

Write the area of each coloured shape.

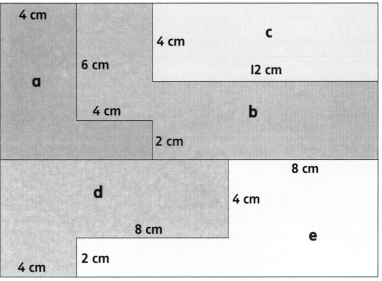

15

Area

Write the area of each triangle.

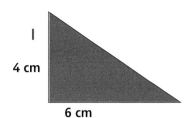

I

4 cm

6 cm

1. $4 \times 6 = 24$
$\frac{1}{2}$ of $24 = 12$ cm^2

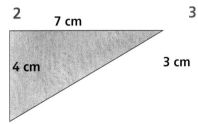

2

7 cm

4 cm

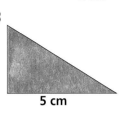

3

3 cm

5 cm

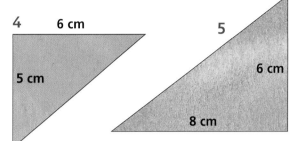

4

6 cm

5 cm

5

6 cm

8 cm

Copy each shape. Write the total area.

6.

5

4   a

b

5   5

a. $4 \times 5 = 20$
b. $4 \times 5 = 20$
$\frac{1}{2}$ of $20 = 10$

Area $= 30$ cm^2

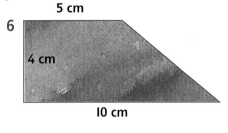

6

5 cm

4 cm

10 cm

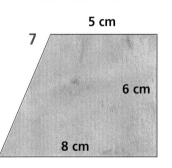

7

5 cm

6 cm

8 cm

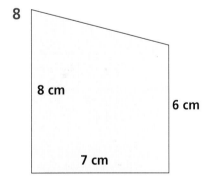

8

8 cm

6 cm

7 cm

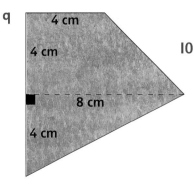

q

4 cm

4 cm

8 cm

4 cm

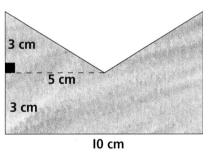

10

3 cm

5 cm

3 cm

10 cm

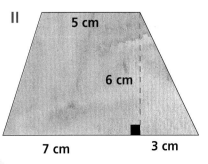

11

5 cm

6 cm

7 cm   3 cm

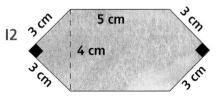

12

3 cm   5 cm   3 cm

4 cm

3 cm   3 cm

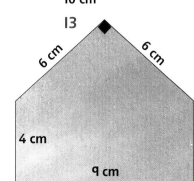

13

6 cm   6 cm

4 cm

q cm

Area

Write the total area of each triangle.

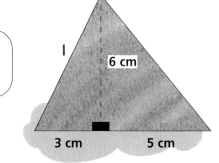

1. $3 \times 6 = 18$
$\frac{1}{2}$ of $18 = 9$
$5 \times 6 = 30$
$\frac{1}{2}$ of $30 = 15$
$9 + 15 = 24 \text{ cm}^2$

2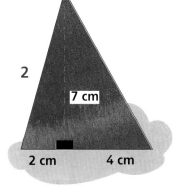

3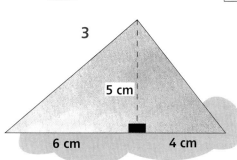

4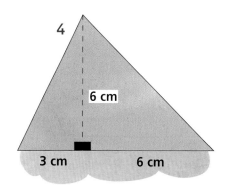

5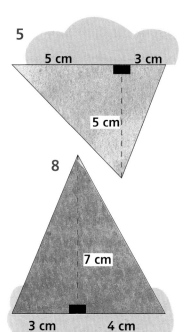

6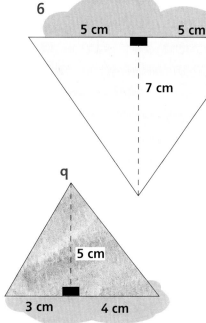

7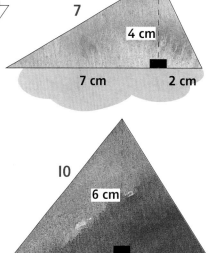

8

9

10

Explore

Draw around different 2-d shapes.

Divide each into triangles and rectangles.

Measure the sides, then find the total area.

Area

Find the area of each circle by counting squares.

Check by calculation.

1. $A = 28\,cm^2$
$3 \times 3 = 9$
$A = 3 \times 9 = 27\,cm^2$

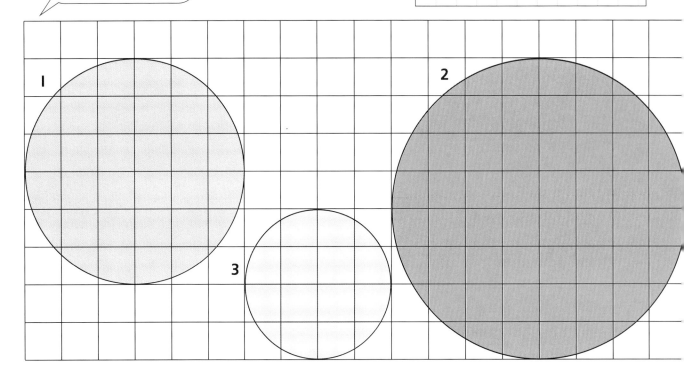

1

2

3

Write the area of each item.

4

r = 5 cm

4. $5 \times 5 = 25$
$A = 3 \times 25 = 75\,cm^2$

5

r = 6 cm

6

r = 1 cm

7

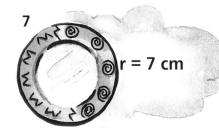

r = 7 cm

8

r = 10 cm

9

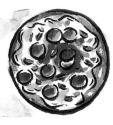

r = 9 cm

10

r = 8 cm

Area

Write the area of each fan.

1

r = 6 cm

1. $6 \times 6 = 36$
$3 \times 36 = 108$
$A = \frac{1}{2}$ of $108 = 54\,cm^2$

2

r = 8 cm

3

r = 10 cm

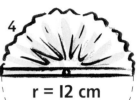

4

r = 12 cm

5

r = 7 cm

6

r = 9 cm

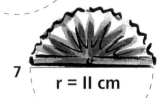

7

r = 11 cm

Write the area of each pizza slice.

8

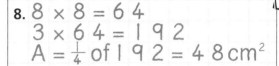

r = 8 cm

8. $8 \times 8 = 64$
$3 \times 64 = 192$
$A = \frac{1}{4}$ of $192 = 48\,cm^2$

9

r = 10 cm

10

r = 12 cm

11

r = 9 cm

Write the radii of circles with these areas.

12

12 cm²

12. $12 \div 3 = 4$
$4 = 2 \times 2$
$r = 2\,cm$

13

48 cm²

14

27 cm²

15

75 cm²

16

300 cm²

19

triangle   **circle**   **square**   **rectangle**   **pentagon**   **hexagon**

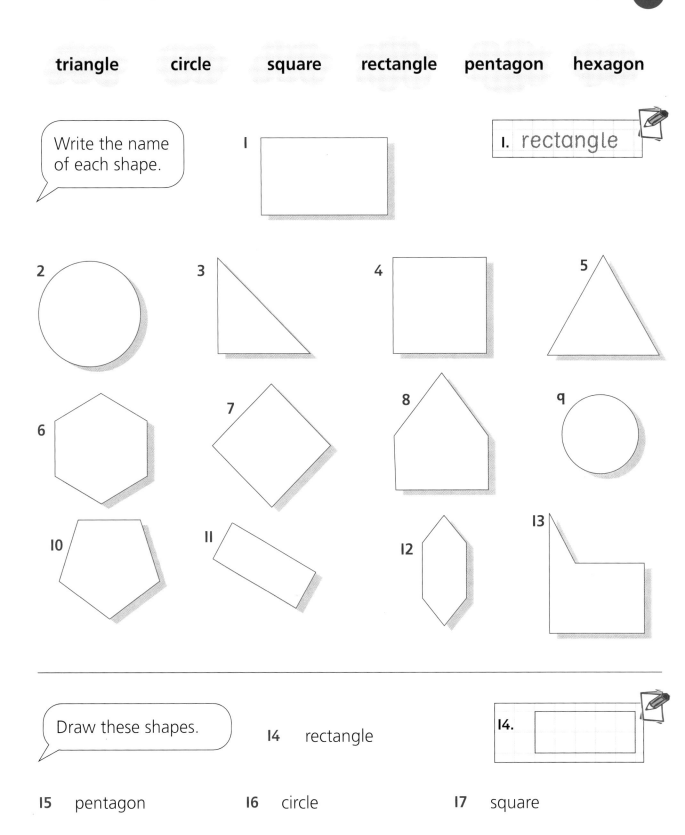

Write the name of each shape.

1. rectangle

Draw these shapes.

14   rectangle

14.

15   pentagon   16   circle   17   square

18   hexagon   19   triangle   20   octagon

Naming shapes

square   rectangle   parallelogram   rhombus   trapezium

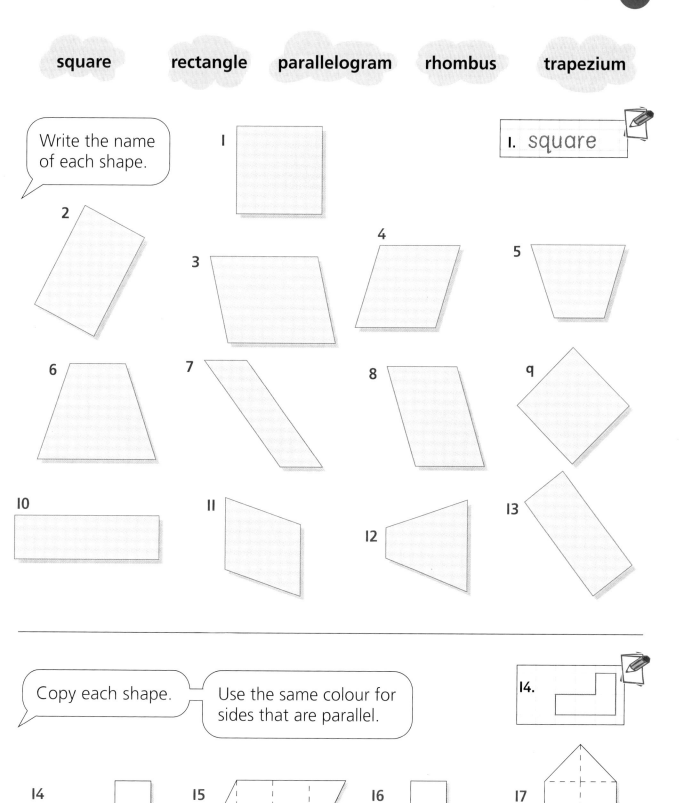

Write the name of each shape.

1. square

Copy each shape.   Use the same colour for sides that are parallel.

Trapeziums

> Are these trapeziums?

I. no

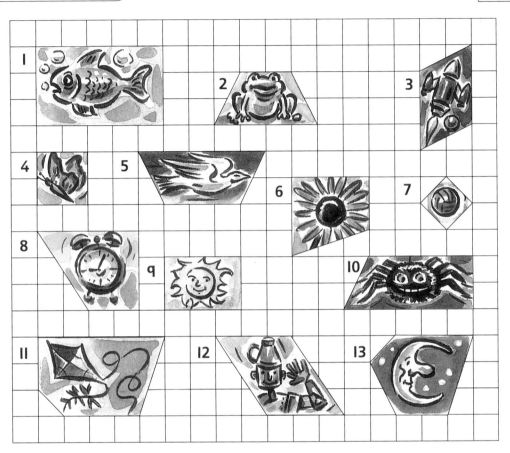

> Write the names of the shapes that are not trapeziums.

Ia. rectangle

Explore

Cut a rectangle from card.

Mark a point on the long side and draw a line to each corner.

Cut out the 3 triangles.

Explore the shapes you can make by joining 2 or 3 triangles.

Draw and name each one.

Quadrilaterals

 Are these quadrilaterals?

 1. no

1 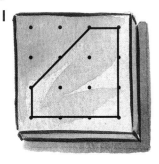	**2** 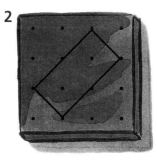	**3** 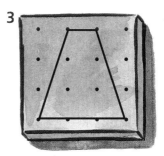	**4** 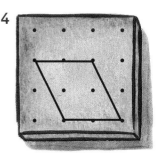
5 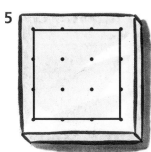	**6** 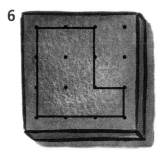	**7** 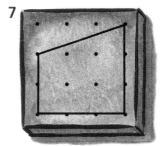	**8** 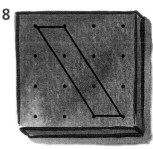
q 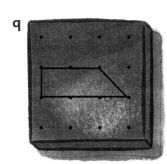	**10** 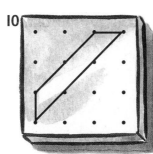	**11** 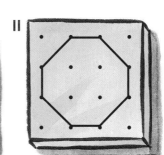	**12** 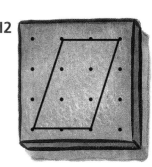

 Write the name of each shape.

1a. pentagon

Explore

Use a 3 x 3 geoboard (or spotty paper).

Make different quadrilaterals.

It is possible to make 16 different quadrilaterals altogether.

How many can you make?

Draw and name each one.

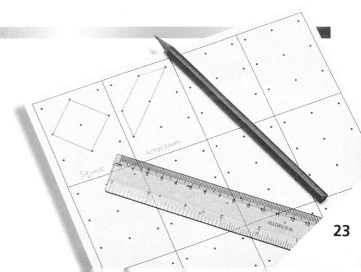

Circles

Measure the radius of each circle.

I. r = 2·5 cm

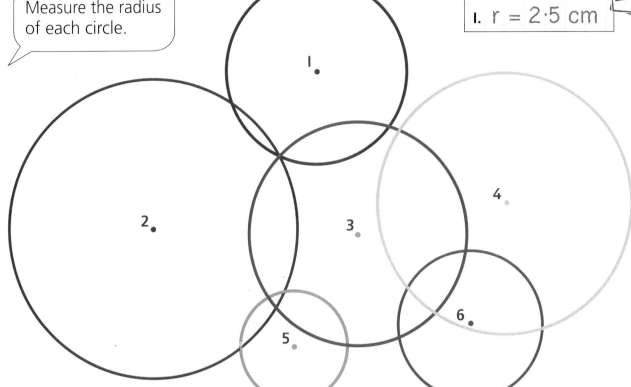

Write the diameter and approximate circumference of each.

Ia. d = 5 cm
    c = 15 cm

Write the approximate circumferences of these.

7. c = 9 cm

7

d = 3 cm

8

r = 4 cm

q
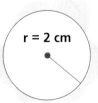
r = 2 cm

I0
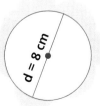
d = 8 cm

II
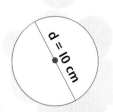
d = 10 cm

I2

r = 7 cm

I3
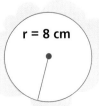
r = 8 cm

I4
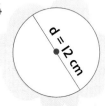
d = 12 cm

24

Circles

Write the approximate diameter and radius of each.

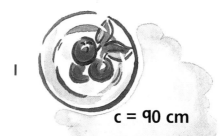

1   c = 90 cm

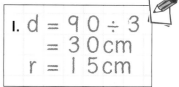

1. d = 90 ÷ 3
    = 30 cm
  r = 15 cm

2  c = 48 cm

3 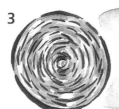 c = 60 cm

4  c = 7·5 cm

5   c = 75 cm

6   c = 15 cm

7   c = 45 cm

Write the approximate length of each arc.

8   5 cm

8. d = 10 cm
   c = 30 cm
  arc = 15 cm

9   4 cm

10    7 cm

11   6 cm

12   14 cm

13   60°   10 cm

14   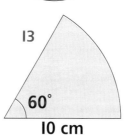 20 cm

Write the perimeter of each shape.

8a. p = 10 + 15 = 25 cm

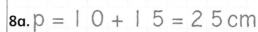

Circles

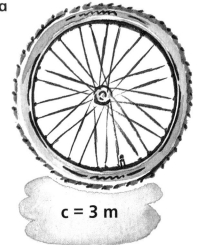

a

c = 3 m

b

c = 2 m

c

$d = \frac{1}{3}$ m

> Write approximately how many times each wheel will turn if it travels:

1   30 m

1a. 3 0 ÷ 3 = 1 0 times

2   15 m   **3**   9 m   **4**   150 m   **5**   3 km

6   1·5 km   **7**   45 m   **8**   60 m   **9**   90 m

> Write approximately how far each wheel will travel if it turns:

10   twice

10a. 2 × 3 = 6 m

11   10 times   **12**   4 times   **13**   100 times   **14**   20 times   **15**   1000 times

 **Explore**

Draw a circle inside a square.

Cut the square into 4 equal tiles.

Investigate different patterns you can make by joining the 4 tiles in a large square.

Naming shapes

cone   **pyramid**   **cuboid**   **cube**   **prism**   **cylinder**

Write the name of each shape.

A

A. cuboid

B   C   D

E   F   G

H   I   J

Write the number of vertices for:

1   H

I. 5

2   G   **3**   B   **4**   A   **5**   I   **6**   D

Write which shapes have:

7   6 edges

7. B

8   6 vertices, 9 edges   **9**   18 edges   **10**   5 vertices

11   7 vertices, 12 edges   **12**   10 vertices   **13**   15 edges

27

3-d shapes

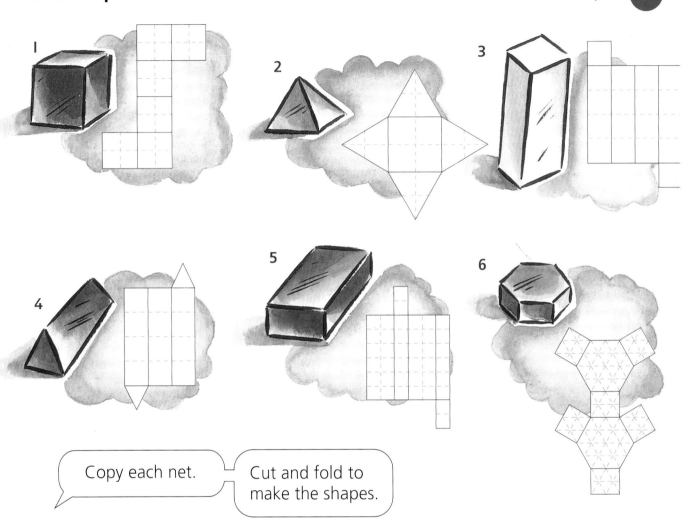

Copy each net.

Cut and fold to make the shapes.

Colour and describe the pairs of parallel faces for each shape.

1. cube: 3 pairs of squares

Explore

Draw on squared paper some different nets of cubes.

Colour the faces so that when the cubes are built, parallel faces are the same colour.

Build the cubes to test them.

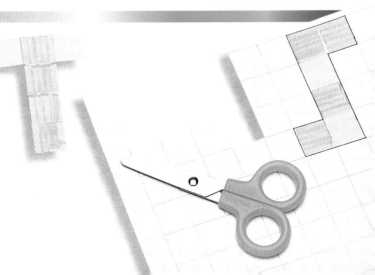

Symmetry

Do these shapes have line symmetry?

 1

I. yes

2

3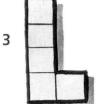

4

5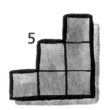

6

7

8

q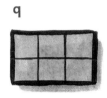

10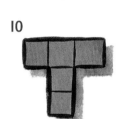

II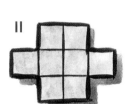

12

13

Copy each shape that has line symmetry. Draw all the lines of symmetry.

Ia.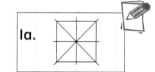

Explore

Use a 3 × 3 geoboard (or spotty paper).

Make shapes that are symmetrical about this line:

How many different shapes can you make? Draw them.

Repeat for a different line of symmetry:

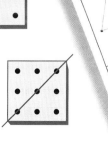

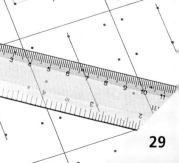

29

Symmetry

Write the order of rotational symmetry for each shape.

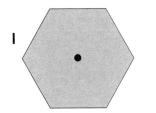

1

2

3

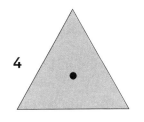

4

5

6

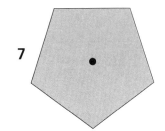

7

8

9

10

1. 6

A	B	C	D	E	F	G	H	I	J	K	L	M
N	O	P	Q	R	S	T	U	V	W	X	Y	Z

Which of these capital letters have rotational symmetry?

For each letter that does, write its order of rotational symmetry.

II. H,

IIa. H → order 2

Symmetry

> Which shapes have line symmetry but not rotational symmetry?

I. B,

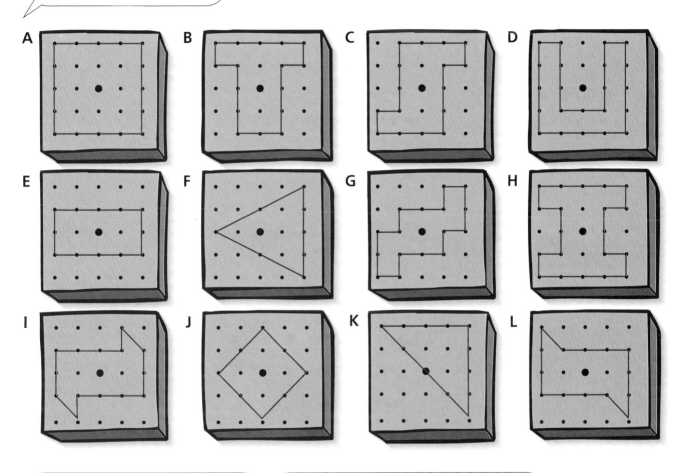

> Which have line symmetry and rotational symmetry?

> Which have rotational symmetry but not line symmetry?

 **Explore**

Draw shapes on squared paper by joining 5 squares edge to edge.

There are 12 different possible shapes. Can you find them?

Find which shapes have:
a line symmetry – draw the lines of symmetry,
b rotational symmetry – mark the centres of rotation.

31

Types of angle

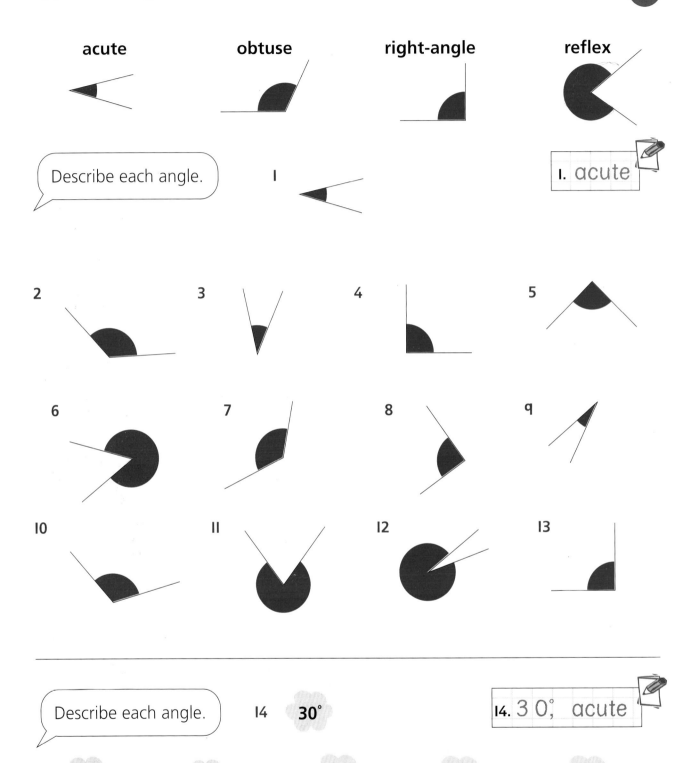

acute **obtuse** **right-angle** **reflex**

Describe each angle.

I

I. acute

2

3

4

5

6

7

8

q

10

II

12

13

Describe each angle. 14   **30°**

14. 3 0° acute

15 **90°** 16 **10°** 17 **120°** 18 **60°** 19 **115°**

20 **190°** 21 **100°** 22 **80°** 23 **240°** 24 **5°**

Types of angle

> Describe each angle.

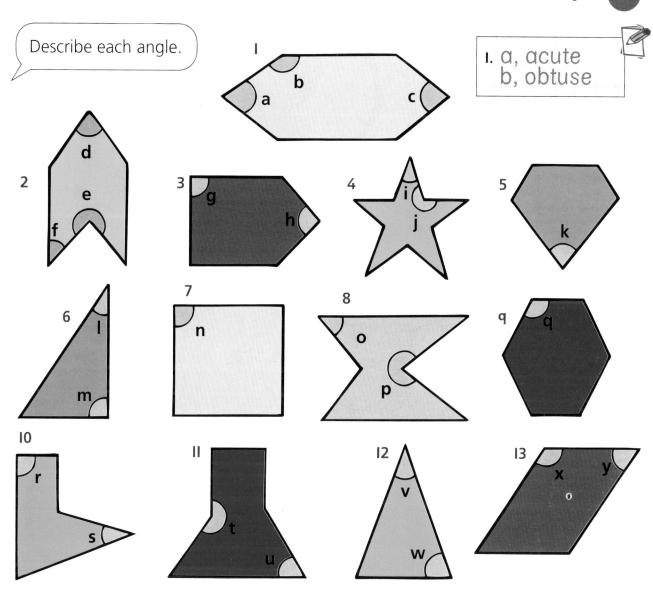

I. a, acute
b, obtuse

Explore

Draw a hexagon with 1 reflex angle.

Draw a hexagon with 2 reflex angles.

Draw an octagon with 3 reflex angles.

Explore different polygons and their number of reflex angles.

Types of angle

Describe each angle.

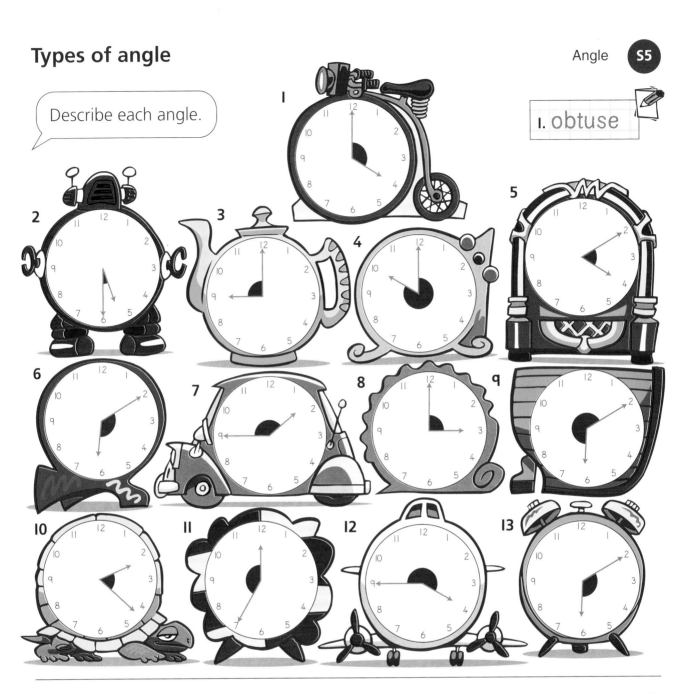

1. obtuse

Describe each clockwise angle of turn.

14. acute

14 N to NE	**15** S to W	**16** SW to NW
17 E to SE	**18** NE to W	**19** N to W
20 NW to SW	**21** E to NE	**22** S to NW

34

Angles

Write the missing angle.

I

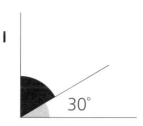 30°

2
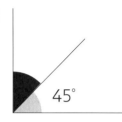 45°

3
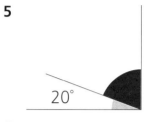 40°

4
30°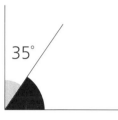

5
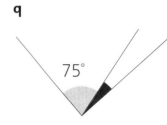 20°

6
35°

7
10°

8
 35°

q
75°

Write the missing angle.

10
 35°

II
 85°

12
50°

13
80°

14
140°

15
120°

16
30°

17
 10°

18
45°

19
135°

Angles

Write the missing angle.

I. 60°

1
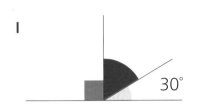
30°

2
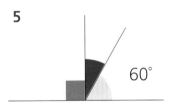
40°

3
20°
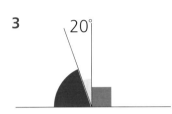

4
25°
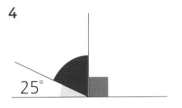

5
60°
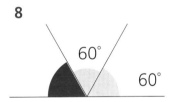

6
35°
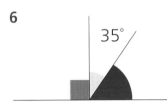

7
50°
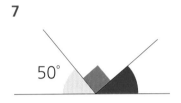

8
60° 60°

q
45° 30°

10
50° 60°

Write the missing angle.

II. 125°

11 145° 90°

12 80° 170°

13 175° 85°

14 80° 160°

15 180° 75°

16 95° 135°

17 190° 45°

18 60° 170°

Angles

> Write the missing angles.

1

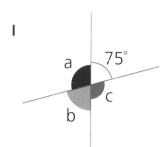

1. b = 7 5°
   a = 1 0 5°
   c = 1 0 5°

2

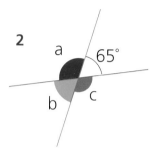

3

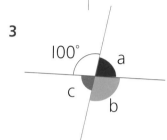

4

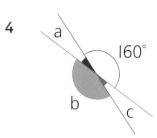

5

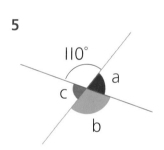

6

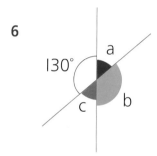

7

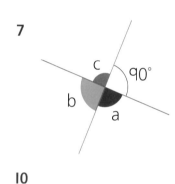

8

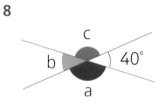

9

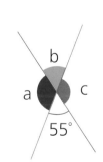

10

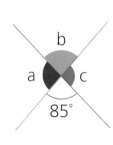

Explore

Draw a straight line.

Draw a second straight line that crosses the first.

Measure one angle, then calculate the others.

Measure to check.

Types of triangle

Write acute-angled or right-angled for each sticker.

1. right-angled

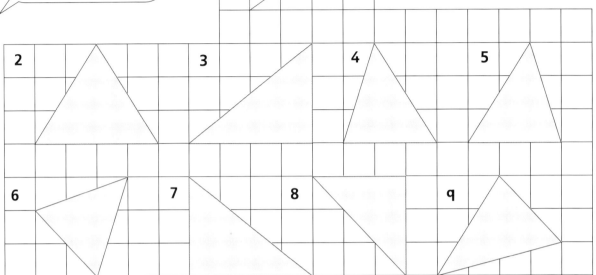

Copy and complete the table.

acute-angled	obtuse-angled	right-angled
A		

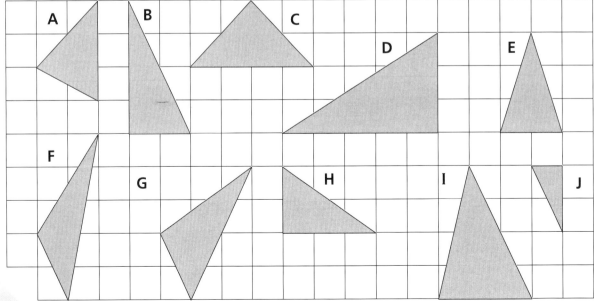

Types of triangle

Draw 3 large triangles.

Measure the angles of each.

Write obtuse-angled, acute-angled or right-angled.

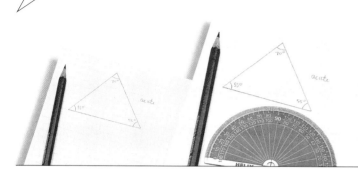

A protractor

Write acute-angled, obtuse-angled or right-angled.

I. right-angled

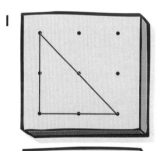
1

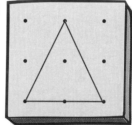
2

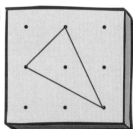
3

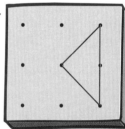
4

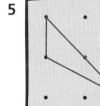
5

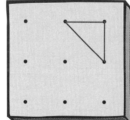
6

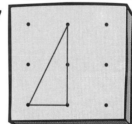
7

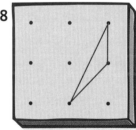
8

 **Explore**

Right-angled triangles tessellate.
They fit together with no gaps.

Investigate for acute-angled triangles.
Investigate for obtuse-angled triangles.

Angles of a triangle

Write the missing angle.

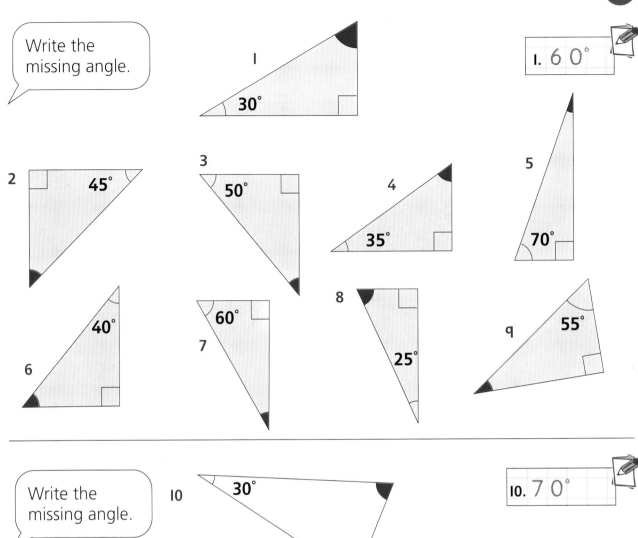

1. 60°

Write the missing angle.

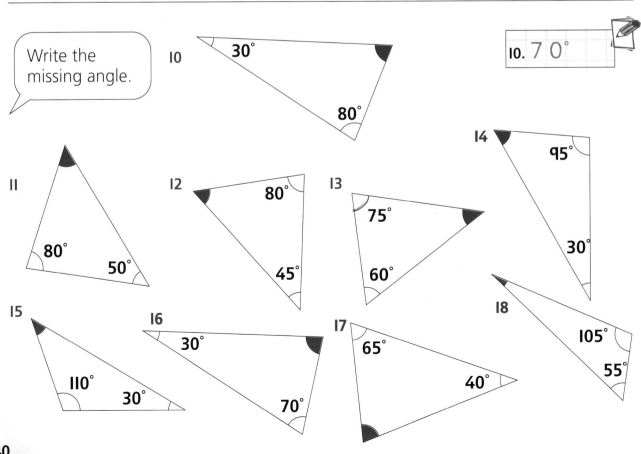

10. 70°

Angles of a triangle

Measure the angles of each triangle.

Find the angle total for each.

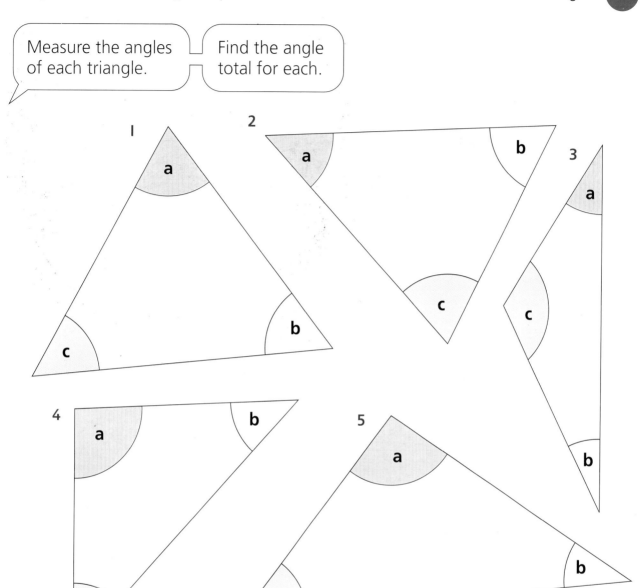

Draw 5 large triangles.

Measure the angles of each.

Find the angle total for each.

A protractor

41

Types of triangle

Write isosceles or equilateral for each.

1. isosceles

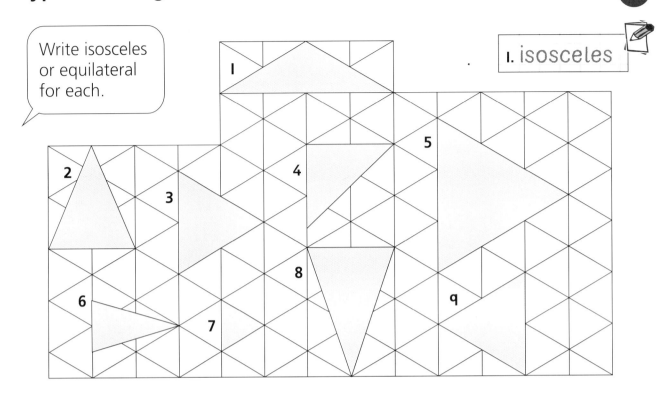

Copy and complete the table.

isosceles	equilateral	scalene
A		

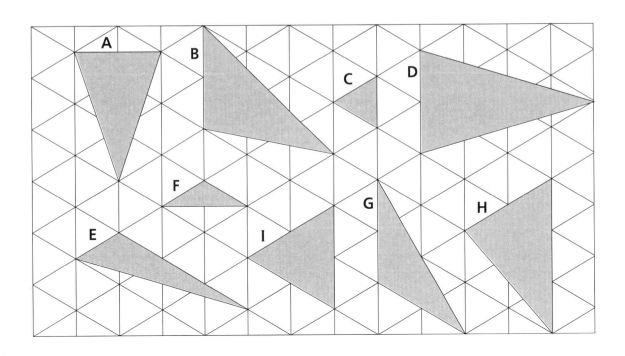

42

Types of triangle

Write the missing angles in these isosceles triangles.

I. a = 6 5°, b = 6 5°

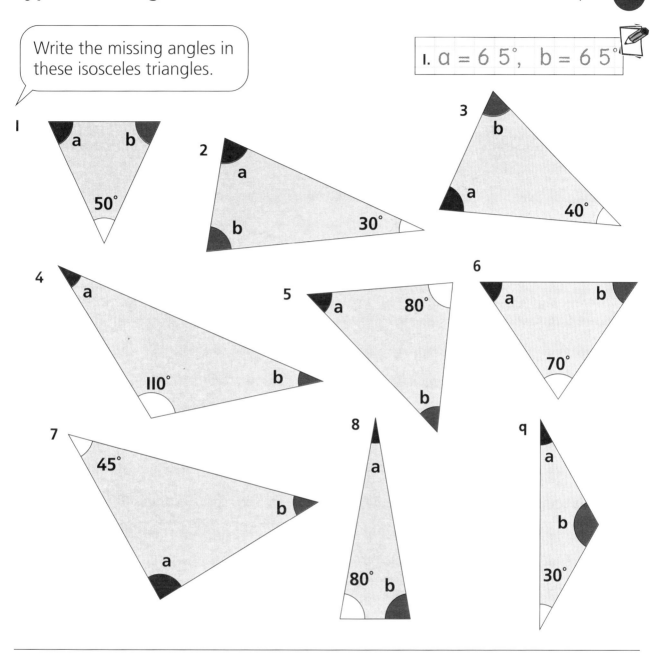

Draw 3 large isosceles triangles.

Measure the sides and angles.

A protractor

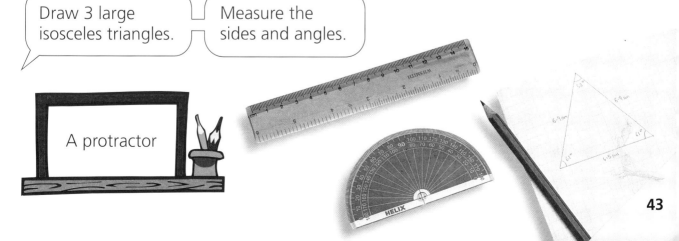

Coordinates

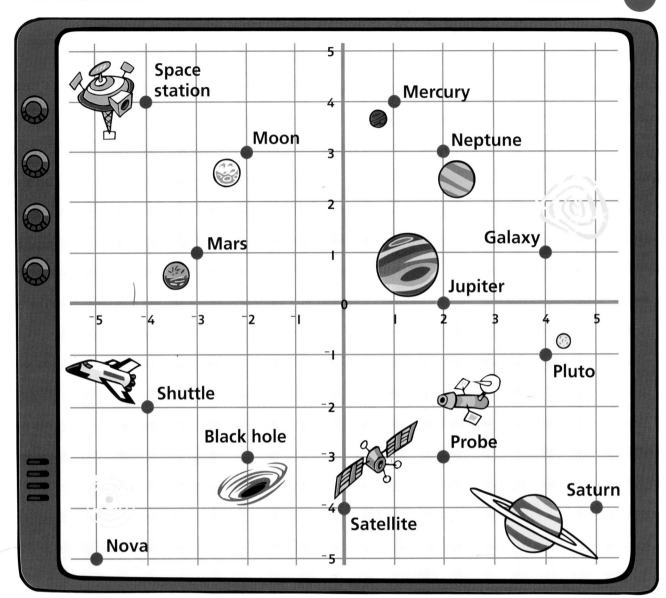

Write the coordinates of these.

1 Shuttle

1. (⁻4, ⁻2)

2 Probe   3 Moon   4 Neptune

5 Space station   6 Nova   7 Galaxy

Write what is at these coordinates.

8 (1, 4)

8. Mercury

9 (⁻3, 1)   10 (⁻2, ⁻3)   11 (2, 0)

12 (4, ⁻1)   13 (0, ⁻4)   14 (5, ⁻4)

Coordinates

Write the coordinates of the stars in each constellation.

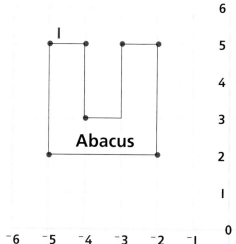

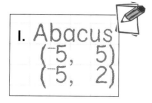

I. Abacus
(⁻5, 5)
(⁻5, 2)

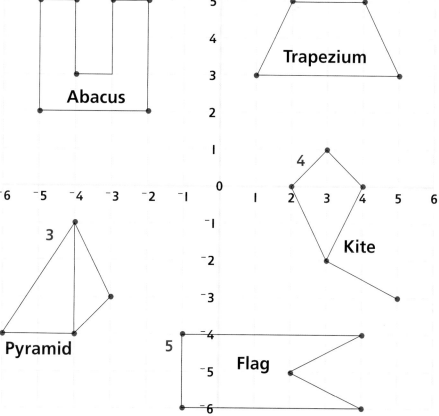

Draw a square coordinate grid from ⁻5 to 5.

Plot each set of points to make a shape.

Name each shape.

6
(1, 5)   (3, 3)
(1, 1)   (⁻1, 3)

7
(3, 4)   (5, ⁻1)
(0, ⁻1)

8
(2, ⁻2)   (⁻2, ⁻2)
(0, ⁻3)   (⁻3, ⁻3)

9
(⁻5, ⁻5)   (⁻3, ⁻3)
(2, ⁻4)   (2, 5)

10
(⁻2, 4)   (⁻4, 2)
(⁻4, 0)   (⁻2, ⁻2)

11
(5, ⁻2)   (5, ⁻5)
(3, ⁻4)

45

Coordinates

Write the coordinates of the vertices of each shape.

1. blue (4,1) (2,2) (4,5) (2,4)

1

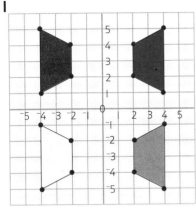

2

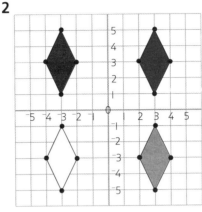

3

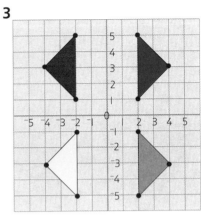

4

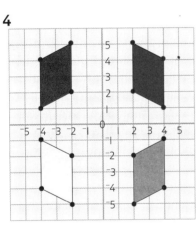

5

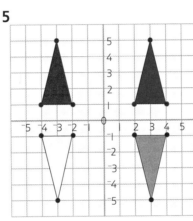

6

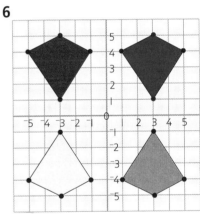

Draw 3 of your own coordinate grids.

Draw sets of reflected shapes.

Write the coordinates of the vertices.

 **Explore**

Draw a square coordinate grid from ⁻5 to 5.

Plot lots of points where the first coordinate is larger than the second: (4, 2), (3, ⁻2), ...

What do you notice about their positions?

Repeat for points where the first coordinate is smaller than the second.

Pie charts

The pie charts show the types of film and programme liked by 8 children.

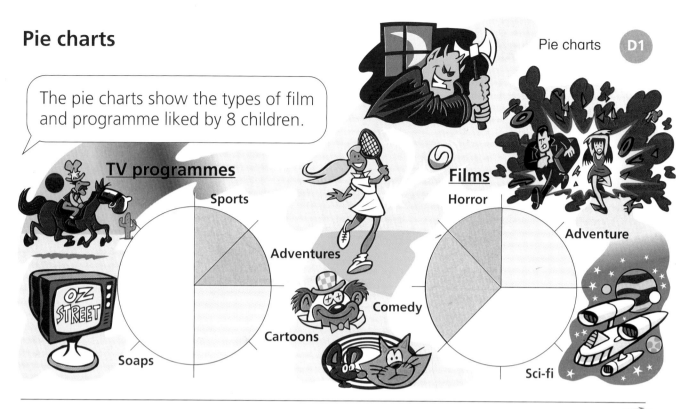

TV programmes

Sports

Adventures

Soaps

Cartoons

Comedy

Films

Horror

Adventure

Sci-fi

How many children liked:

| | Sports programmes? | I. |

2 Horror films?   **3** Cartoon programmes?   **4** Adventure films?

5 Comedy films?   **6** Sci-fi films?   **7** Soap programmes?

What was the most popular type of: **8** film?   **q** programme?

What was the least popular type of: **10** film?   **11** programme?

What fraction of children liked: **12** Soaps?   **13** Sports?   **14** Comedy?

15 Horror?   **16** Cartoons?   **17** Sci-fi?   **18** Adventure films?

Choose 8 children.

Draw 2 pie charts to show their favourite types of film and TV programme.

Write about the pie charts.

Pie chart paper

47

Pie charts

16 children voted for their favourite sport.

Our favourite sports

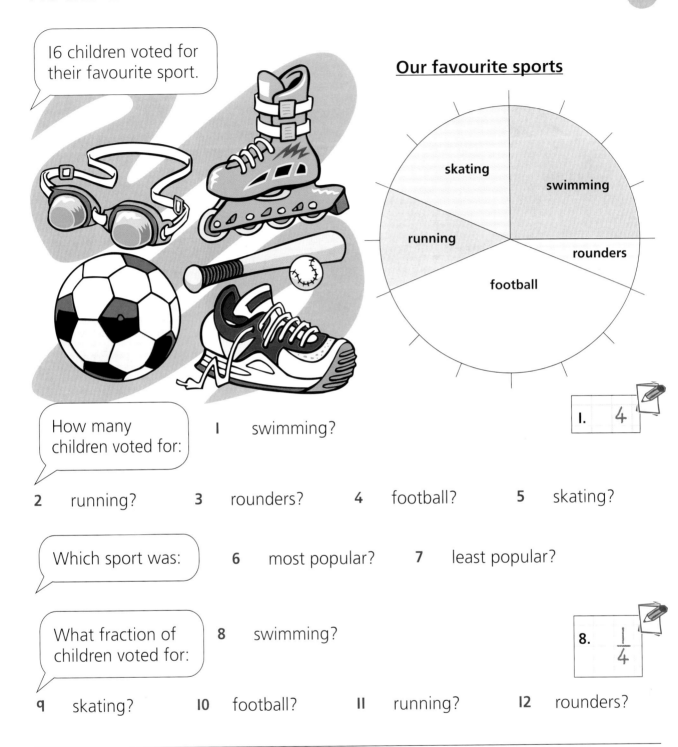

skating	swimming
running	rounders
football	

| I. | 4 |

How many children voted for:

I   swimming?

2   running?   3   rounders?   4   football?   5   skating?

Which sport was: 6   most popular?   7   least popular?

What fraction of children voted for: 8   swimming?

| 8. | $\frac{1}{4}$ |

9   skating?   10   football?   11   running?   12   rounders?

Roll a dice 16 times.

Draw a pie chart to show how many times each number was thrown.

Write about the pie chart.

Pie chart paper
A dice

Line graphs

The graph shows the changing temperature in a classroom.

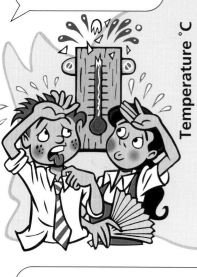

Temperature in our classroom

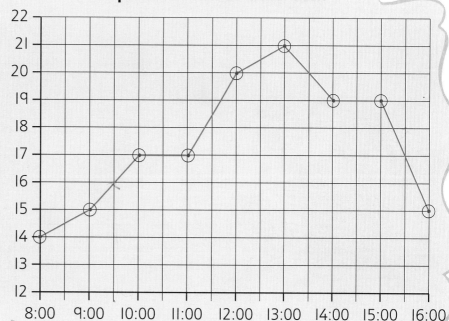

What is the temperature at:

| 1 | 9 o'clock? | I. | 15°C |

2   1 o'clock?   3   12 o'clock?   4   10 o'clock?   5   4 o'clock?

6   2 o'clock?   7   half-past 9?   8   half-past 3?   9   half-past 11?

At what time is the temperature:

10   15°C?   11   17°C?   12   20°C?

13   16°C?   14   19°C?   15   18°C?

16   at its warmest?   17   at its coldest?

Write a time when:

18   the room is getting warmer   19   the room is getting colder

---

What happens to the temperature between:

20   8:00 and 10:00?   21   12:00 and 14:00?

22   13:00 and 16:00?   23   10:00 and 11:00?   24   11:00 and 13:00?

49

Line graphs

The graph shows the number of people watching television during one night.

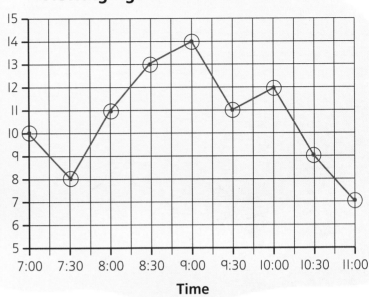

Viewing figures for Channel 9

Number of viewers (thousands)

Time

How many people are watching at:

1 8 o'clock?   1. 11,000

2 10 o'clock?   **3** half-past 7?   **4** half-past 8?   **5** 7 o'clock?

6 half-past 10?   **7** half-past 9?   **8** 11 o'clock?   **9** 9 o'clock?

At what time are this number of people watching?

10 10 000   **11** 14 000

12 7000   **13** 9000   **14** 8000   **15** 13 000

Write 2 times when the number of viewers:

16 is rising   **17** is falling

What happens to the number of viewers between:

18 7:00 and 8:00?   **19** 10:00 and 11:00?

20 8:00 and 9:00?   **21** 9:00 and 10:00?   **22** 9:30 and 10:30?

Line graphs

The table shows the height of a balloon.

Time	9:00	10:00	11:00	12:00	13:00	14:00	15:00	16:00	17:00
Height (m)	0	40	70	50	80	100	70	80	60

Draw a line graph to show the changing height of the balloon.

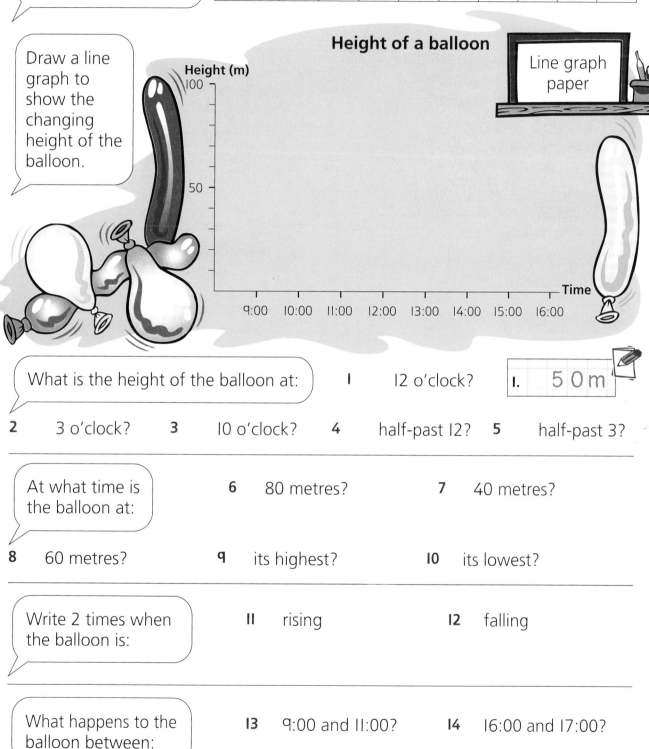

Height of a balloon

Line graph paper

What is the height of the balloon at:

1 12 o'clock?

1. 50m

2 3 o'clock? **3** 10 o'clock? **4** half-past 12? **5** half-past 3?

At what time is the balloon at:

6 80 metres? **7** 40 metres?

8 60 metres? **9** its highest? **10** its lowest?

Write 2 times when the balloon is:

11 rising **12** falling

What happens to the balloon between:

13 9:00 and 11:00? **14** 16:00 and 17:00?

15 12:00 and 14:00? **16** 10:00 and 12:00? **17** 14:00 and 16:00?

51

Conversion graphs

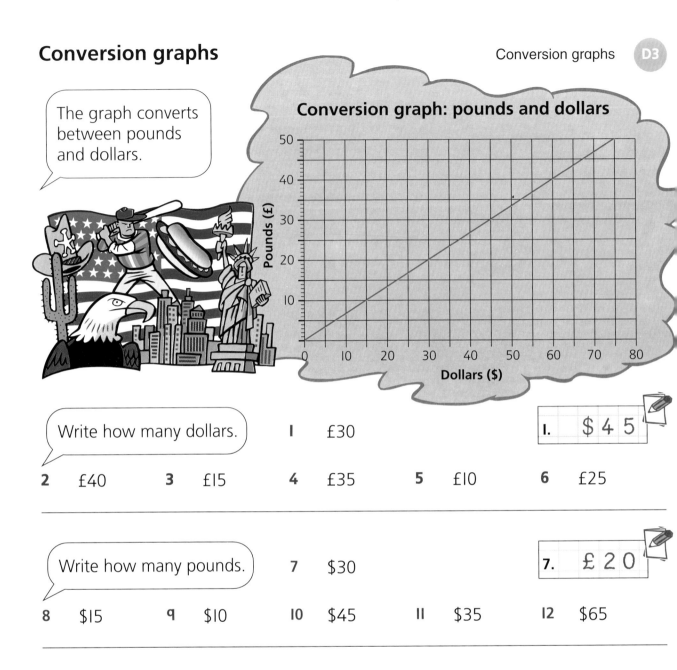

The graph converts between pounds and dollars.

Conversion graph: pounds and dollars

Write how many dollars.

I   £30

I. $ 4 5

2   £40   **3**   £15   **4**   £35   **5**   £10   **6**   £25

Write how many pounds.

7 $30

7.   £ 2 0

8 $15   **q** $10   **10** $45   **II** $35   **12** $65

Draw a graph to convert between French francs and pounds.

Let £1 be worth 10 French francs, so £10 is worth 100 French francs.

Plot the point (100, 10), then draw a straight line from (0, 0).

Convert these amounts:

13   20 Fr   **14**   50 Fr

15   80 Fr   **16**   175 Fr

17   115 Fr

Conversion graph: pounds and francs

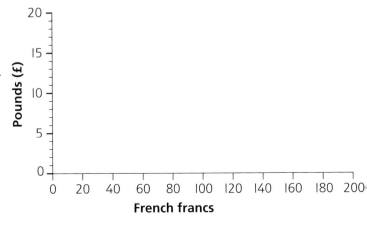

Conversion graphs

Conversion graph: °F and °C

The graph converts between temperatures measured in Fahrenheit and Centigrade.

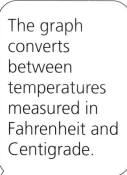

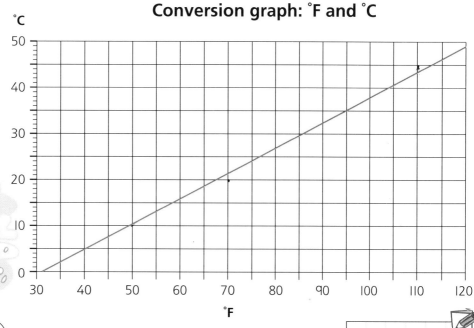

Write each temperature in °F.

| | 30°C

I. 86°F

2 20°C   **3** 40°C   **4** 15°C   **5** 35°C   **6** 25°C

Write each temperature in °C.

7 80°F

7. 27°C

8 50°F   **9** 70°F   **10** 95°F   **11** 65°F   **12** 110°F

These are the average temperatures in Sunville.

Month	Jan	Feb	Mar	Apr	May	Jun	Jul	Aug	Sep	Oct	Nov	Dec
Temperature °C	2°	5°	10°	16°	20°	21°	25°	28°	26°	18°	9°	6°

Draw a new table with each temperature in °F.

53

Conversion graphs

The graph converts between miles and kilometres.

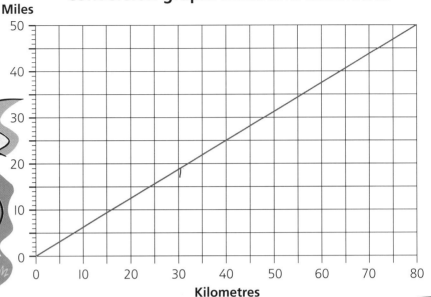

Conversion graph: miles and kilometres

Write how many kilometres.

| 1 | 20 miles | **1.** 3 2 km |

| 2 | 30 miles | **3** | 50 miles | **4** | 15 miles | **5** | 25 miles | **6** | 45 miles |

Write how many miles.

| 7 | 40 km | **7.** 2 5 miles |

| 8 | 60 km | **9** | 20 km | **10** | 15 km | **11** | 55 km | **12** | 75 km |

Write each speed in miles per hour.

| 13 | 80 km/h | **13.** 5 0 mph |

| 14 | 65 km/h | **15** | 25 km/h | **16** | 50 km/h | **17** | 30 km/h | **18** | 70 km/h |

Draw a new table with each distance in miles.

From Longridge	To Backton	To Farley	To Weybridge	To Johnston	To Midwich	To Hayes
km	47	32	28	53	76	59

Grouped frequencies

These are the heights of 30 children.

| 109 cm | 111 cm | 98 cm | 118 cm | 108 cm | 114 cm |

| 122 cm | 101 cm | 106 cm | 112 cm | 104 cm | 113 cm | 91 cm | 107 cm | 128 cm | 94 cm | 113 cm | 110 cm |

| 119 cm | 102 cm | 108 cm | 116 cm | 102 cm | 96 cm | 111 cm | 105 cm | 114 cm | 95 cm | 123 cm | 112 cm |

Copy and complete the tally chart to show how many heights are in each group.

Height (cm)	Tallies	Frequency
90-95		
95-100		
100-105		

Draw a graph to show the results.

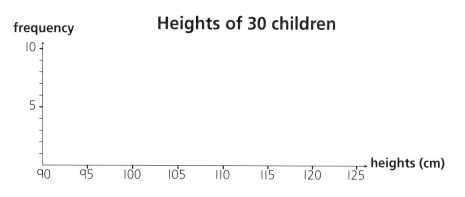

Heights of 30 children

frequency

heights (cm)

How many children have heights:

1 between 90 and 95 cm?

2 between 100 and 105 cm?

3 between 115 and 120 cm?

4 between 110 and 115 cm?

5 between 100 and 110 cm?

6 between 95 and 115 cm?

7 100 cm or more?

8 less than 105 cm?

Grouped frequencies

These are the race times in seconds, for the sack race.

14.3 15.5 12.1 18.4 13.9 16.3 15.5 13.6 15.0

19.1 11.8 14.4 17.0 12.7 14.9 17.8 16.9 14.7

13.2 16.1 15.3 17.5 19.6 15.8 14.6 13.8 15.9

Draw a frequency table to show how many times are in the intervals 10-12, 12-14, 14-16, 16-18, 18-20.

Time	Frequency
10-12	
12-14	
14-16	

Draw a graph to show the results.

Sack race times

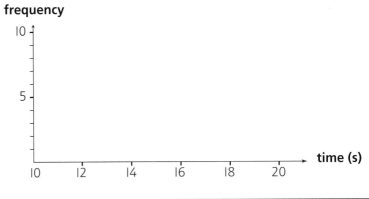

How many ran the race:

1 between 12 and 14 s?

2 between 16 and 18 s?

3 between 10 and 12 s?

4 between 14 and 16 s?

5 between 12 and 16 s?

6 between 14 and 18 s?

7 in 14 s or more?

8 in less than 16 s?

Grouped frequencies

 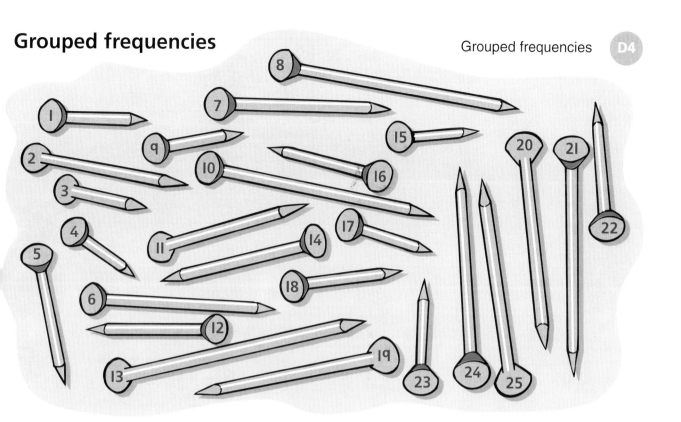

Measure each nail in millimetres.

Write each length in centimetres.

1. 3·1 cm

Group the lengths and draw a frequency table.

Lengths (cm)	Frequency

Draw a graph to show the results.

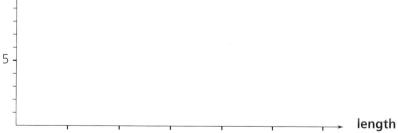

Invent 5 questions about the graph.

Write the answers to your questions.

The mean

> Teams of 5 children tried to score penalties.

> Each child had 10 shots.

Blue team	5, 7, 3, 4, 6	White team	2, 4, 3, 5, 6
Red team	7, 10, 3, 8, 7	Green team	6, 6, 8, 3, 7
Yellow team	6, 7, 1, 3, 8	Orange team	1, 5, 6, 4, 9

> Write the mean score for each team.

1. Blue total = 2 5
   mean: $25 \div 5 = 5$

> These children had 3 turns to knock down 10 skittles.

> Write the mean score for each child.

7. Total = 1 5
   mean: $15 \div 3 = 5$

7   Nancy 5, 7, 3   8   Gary 4, 3, 8   9   Kevin 2, 9, 7

10 Corinna 8, 5, 5   11 Katy 6, 3, 1   12 Tom 3, 0, 9

> Write the mean amount spent at each stall.

13
lucky dip

7p 10p 9p

14p

13. Total = 4 0p
    mean: $40 \div 4 = 1 0p$

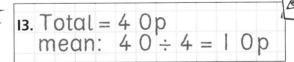

14
coconut shy

2p 5p 3p 5p

8p 7p

15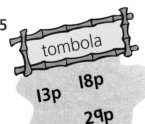
tombola

13p 18p

29p

16
treasure hunt

28p

36p

17
hoopla!

16p 24p

28p 16p

31p

The mode

These are the shoe sizes of children in 2 classes.

Class B1			Class C3		
$2\frac{1}{2}$	3	3	4	$3\frac{1}{2}$	3
4	$3\frac{1}{2}$	2	2	$4\frac{1}{2}$	5
$1\frac{1}{2}$	$2\frac{1}{2}$	3	$4\frac{1}{2}$	3	$3\frac{1}{2}$
$2\frac{1}{2}$	2	3	4	$1\frac{1}{2}$	$2\frac{1}{2}$
3	$1\frac{1}{2}$	4	$3\frac{1}{2}$	4	$3\frac{1}{2}$
$3\frac{1}{2}$	$4\frac{1}{2}$	$2\frac{1}{2}$	$2\frac{1}{2}$	3	3
2	$2\frac{1}{2}$	$3\frac{1}{2}$	5	$3\frac{1}{2}$	2
3	2	3	4	$4\frac{1}{2}$	4
$2\frac{1}{2}$	3	$2\frac{1}{2}$	3	$3\frac{1}{2}$	$3\frac{1}{2}$
$3\frac{1}{2}$	2	3	$3\frac{1}{2}$	$2\frac{1}{2}$	3

For each class draw a frequency table to show how many children wear each size.

Write the modes and how the classes compare.

shoe size	frequency
$1\frac{1}{2}$	
2	
$2\frac{1}{2}$	

Explore

Collect data on the number of letters in children's names in your class.

Draw a frequency table and find the mode.

Before you start, guess what the mode will be.

The median

These are the goals scored by different football teams.

United	4, 2, 1, 0, 3, 2, 0, 1, 3, 4, 5
City	2, 1, 2, 1, 3, 2, 1, 0, 2
Rangers	4, 1, 2, 3, 5, 0, 2, 1, 2, 3, 6
Rovers	3, 5, 3, 2, 4, 1, 3
Town	2, 7, 3, 1, 0, 1, 2, 3, 2, 1, 2
Wanderers	3, 2, 1, 2, 3, 1, 2
Albion	0, 1, 2, 1, 0, 3, 2, 4, 2
Kickers	2, 1, 2, 3, 2, 5, 2, 6, 3, 2, 3

For each team, write the goals scored, in order, from smallest to largest.

Write the median for each team.

1. United: 0,   0,   1,   1,

Explore

Throw two dice 10 times. List the scores.

Calculate the mean, the mode and the median for your scores.

How do they compare?

Repeat several times.

Compare each set of scores.

Probability

> Copy and complete this table for throwing a dice, 1 to 6, showing the probability of:

	Event	Chance	Probability
1	a 2	1 in 6	$\frac{1}{6}$
2	a 5		

1 throwing a 2

2 throwing a 5

3 throwing an odd number

4 throwing more than 3

5 throwing less than 5

6 throwing 2 or more

7 throwing an even number

8 throwing a 7

9 throwing less than 7

0 ├──────────────────────────────┤ 1

> Copy the probability line and mark each of these events along it.

a I will sleep tonight.

b It will rain next week.

c I will eat cheese tomorrow.

d I will be younger tomorrow.

e I will watch TV tonight.

f I will watch a video tonight.

g I will go swimming next month.

h I will be famous one day.

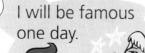

i It will snow tomorrow.

j I will play football next week.

61

Probability

These 10 cubes are put in a bag.

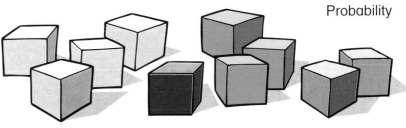

Copy and complete this table for removing a cube, showing the probability of:

	Event	Chance	Probability
1	yellow	4 in 10	$\frac{4}{10}$ or $\frac{2}{5}$
2	red		

1 taking a yellow

2 taking a red

3 taking a green

4 taking a blue

5 taking a red or a yellow

6 taking a green or a blue

7 taking a blue or a red

8 not taking a red

9 taking a pink

10 not taking a blue

11 not taking a green

12 not taking a yellow

Match each event above to a position on this line.

ⓐ ⓑ ⓒ ⓓ ⓔ ⓕ ⓖ ⓗ ⓘ ⓙ ⓚ

0   0·5   1

1a. e

If a cube is taken out and put back 40 times, predict how many times will match each event?

1b. 1 6 out of   4 0

Put the 10 cubes in a bag, taking one out and putting it back 40 times.

Compare the results with your predictions.

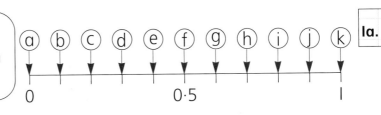

event	prediction	result
yellow		
red		

Probability

Two dice are thrown and the total score is found.

Copy and complete the grid to show all the possible outcomes.

red

green

	1	2	3	4	5	6
1						
2			5			
3						
4	5					
5				10		
6						

Copy and complete this table to show the probability of each total.

How many times does each number appear on the grid?

Event	Chance	Probability
total is 2	1 in 36	$\frac{1}{36}$
total is 3		
total is 4		
total is 5		

Throw two dice 36 times.

Compare the results with the probabilities from above.

Write the results in a new table.

Event	Prediction	Result
total is 2	1	
total is 3		

Probability

Two coins are tossed to see if they land 'heads' or 'tails'.

Copy and complete the table to show all the possible outcomes.

50p	10p
heads	tails

Copy and complete this table to show the probability of each outcome.

Event	Chance	Probability
both heads		
both tails		
one head, one tail		

Toss two coins 24 times.

Compare the results with the probabilities from above.

Write the results in a new table.

Event	Prediction	Result
both heads		
both tails		
one head, one tail		